buzzing!

Discover the poetry in garden minibeasts

Anneliese Emmans Dean

Brambleby Books Ltd.

ISBN 978-1-908241-07-8

First published in 2012 by
BRAMBLEBY BOOKS
Luton, Bedfordshire, UK
www.bramblebybooks.co.uk

Cover design and book layout by Creatix Design Services
Photography by Anneliese Emmans Dean

Printed on FSC paper by
Cambrian Printers, Aberystwyth, UK.

Acknowledgements

A big 'Thank You' to the many people who have
assisted me, encouraged me and opened doors for me
on my *Buzzing!* adventure.

Dedication

To Ma, Pa
and Mike

Contents

About the Author

Anneliese Emmans Dean is a poet, photographer and performer who has won prizes ranging from the Royal Entomological Society's Lesley Goodman Award to the *New Statesman* Limerick Competition.

Anneliese studied Modern and Medieval Languages at Cambridge University. She often performs her humorous poems on BBC radio. Her live *Buzzing!* show is a hit with children and adults up and down the land, from the Edinburgh Fringe to Oxford Playhouse. She also enjoys edu-taining pupils in schools, and grown-ups in groups such as the U3A and WI.

Anneliese's photographs are published in books, calendars, magazines and the scientific literature.

It took Anneliese eight years to take the photos in this book – most of them in and around her small garden on the outskirts of York, a hop, skip and a jump from where she grew up.

Find out more at Anneliese's website:
www.theBigBuzz.biz

Foreword

Are you buzzing? Maybe not yet, but I guarantee that you will be.

Prepare yourself for a fabulous fun-filled flight through the wonderful world of the wiggly, wriggly and giggly.

Anyone who has been to one of Anneliese's award-winning live *Buzzing!* shows will know exactly what I mean. There's a jungle out there, full of the most amazing things, and it's right on your doorstep. Anneliese is the guide that you've been waiting for. You're going on a minibeast safari and you'll be edu-entertain-amazed when she shows you what's lurking at the bottom of your garden.

Through hilarious poems, stunning photographs and factabulous facts, *Buzzing!* drags the outside inside and brings it to life. And best of all, once your curiosity has been well and truly sparked, you'll discover that your journey has only just begun. Spending time in your garden will never be the same again!

Dr Ben Darvill
Chief Executive Officer,
Bumblebee Conservation Trust

The Bumblebee Conservation Trust is a UK charity working towards a vision in which our communities and countryside are rich in bumblebees and colourful flowers, supporting a diversity of wildlife and habitats for everyone to enjoy.

To learn more about the fascinating lives of bumblebees, support our vital conservation work or join online, visit: www.bumblebeeconservation.org

It's Buzzing

It's buzzing in my garden
It's buzzing in yours too
And in the park and on the playing field
It's buzzing – look, it's true.

It's buzzing in the bushes
Buzzing in the trees
Buzzing in the flowers
In the lettuces and peas.

Buzzing underneath your feet
Buzzing in the air
Buzzing round your midriff
Buzzing everywhere.

It's very buzzing busy
In the pages of this book
Eyes and ears on red alert?
Let's go and have a look!

buzzing

busy!

Common Carder Bee

Jane Bond

On Her Majesty's Service

Jane Bond is a bee on a mission
Seeking out pollen with furry precision
Smart, preened, resourceful and keen
She's determined to please her Queen.

Jane Bond has purpose and vision
Committed to finding the finest nutrition
From all the flowers she visits each day
So her Queen can have her way.

Jane Bond is in peak condition
Expertly executes each expedition
As buds unfurl, she angles and curls
To reach their nectar pearls.

Yes, Jane Bond has one goal on her mind
So never forget her dangerous behind
She's a bee on a mission, a bee who can't fail
This is a bee with a sting in her tail!

Bombus pascuorum

BUG BOX

COMMON NAME Common Carder Bee
SCIENTIFIC NAME *Bombus pascuorum*
FAMILY Apidae
ORDER Hymenoptera
CLASS Insecta
PHYLUM Arthropoda
KINGDOM Animalia

ADULTS

SIZE 10–15mm
FAVOURITE FOOD Nectar from flowers
LIKE TO BE Near flowers
SEE THEM March to November

FACTABULOUS!

✫ The Common Carder Bee is a bumblebee.

✫ Only female bumblebees collect pollen, in special 'pollen baskets' on their back legs. (You can see one of Jane Bond's pollen baskets in the photo.)

✫ Jane Bond is a 'worker bee'. All worker bees are female, and they serve their queen bee by taking pollen back to the nest to feed to their younger sisters (and later on, their brothers too).

✫ Only female bumblebees can sting.

Yellow Dung Fly

Dung fly

A heartfelt lament

It's difficult being a dung fly
It would be easy but for my name
If I weren't called a dung fly
I'd be free of this sense of shame.

Maybe I'm just oversensitive
Maybe the others don't care
But being named after cow poo?
I think that's awfully unfair.

Look, this is me on a foxglove
And here, on a Pieris twig
I'm really quite cosmopolitan
But the nomenclaturists don't give a fig.

My Latin name's not much better
In fact, it's even worse:
Scathophaga stercoraria
Not much short of a curse.

Yes OK, I like dung, I admit it
I like it a lot, it's true
But there's more to life than cowpats
There's more to me than poo.

Future parents take note, I implore you
Think hard before naming your child
Choose a name to bring them happiness
Not one that will drive them wild!

Scathophaga stercoraria

BUG BOX

COMMON NAME Yellow Dung Fly
SCIENTIFIC NAME *Scathophaga stercoraria*
FAMILY Scathophagidae
ORDER Diptera
CLASS Insecta
PHYLUM Arthropoda
KINGDOM Animalia

ADULTS

SIZE 8–10mm
FAVOURITE FOOD Insects (that live on or near dung)
LIKE TO BE Near dung!
SEE THEM April to October

FACTABULOUS!

⇨ Male Yellow Dung Flies like to hang out on dung (especially cowpats) to attract a mate.

⇨ Female Yellow Dung Flies lay their eggs on cowpats (and other dung).

Marmalade Hoverfly

Celestia

Who can never quite
make up her mind

I hover hither and thither
I dither and quiver, then sit
For a second then thither and hither again
Then from flower to flower I flit

I hover from sepal to stamen
From stigma to petal to leaf
I hover suspended, then dip and then rise
Then I dash off in search of relief

To a poppy, pink petalled and open
To some lavender there that looks nice
On to a pendulous Fuchsia
Then I'm off again, in a trice

I hover hither and thither
I hover and bother, then sit
For a second then dither and quiver again
Then flit off somewhere else for a bit.

Episyrphus balteatus

BUG BOX

COMMON NAME	Marmalade Hoverfly
SCIENTIFIC NAME	*Episyrphus balteatus*
FAMILY	Syrphidae
ORDER	Diptera
CLASS	Insecta
PHYLUM	Arthropoda
KINGDOM	Animalia

ADULTS

SIZE	9–12mm
FAVOURITE FOOD	Nectar and pollen
LIKE TO BE	Where there are flowers
SEE THEM	March to early November

FACTABULOUS!

✥ Bees and wasps have four wings. Hoverflies have only two wings.

✥ Hoverflies are in the order Diptera.

✥ The word Diptera comes from the Greek *di*, which means 'two', and *ptera*, which means 'wings'.

✥ Yellow Dung Flies (see page 14) are also in the order Diptera.

Bee-fly

Herbert

Who's not what he seems

Gotcha! Admit it!
You thought I was a bee
Buzzing round your garden
Feasting for free.

You thought you'd keep your distance
Not wanting to be stung
Just what I intended
Job well done!

Bombus, Bombus
That's not me
I'm Bombylius, Bombylius
Tee hee hee!

Bombylius major

BUG BOX

COMMON NAME	Bee-fly
SCIENTIFIC NAME	*Bombylius major*
FAMILY	Bombyliidae
ORDER	Diptera
CLASS	Insecta
PHYLUM	Arthropoda
KINGDOM	Animalia

ADULTS

SIZE	12–16mm
FAVOURITE FOOD	Nectar from flowers
LIKE TO BE	Near flowers
SEE THEM	March to June

FACTABULOUS!

- The Bee-fly is a bee mimic. It looks very like a bee, but it isn't one.

- The Bee-fly always has its long proboscis (its tongue) stuck out. This is one of the ways you can tell it isn't a bee.

- Also, bees have four wings, but Bee-flies have only two.

- So Bee-flies are in the order Diptera (along with hoverflies – see page 16). Bees are in a different order – Hymenoptera.

Common Wasp

Wasp

Crafty!

We wasps are rather clever
We wasps are rather smart
We nibble up your furniture
And turn it into art.

We're engineers-cum-artists
And what we like the best
Is swirling different colours
Round our perfect paper nests.

Yes, you heard right, we said 'paper'
We told you we're not daft
Aeons before you humans
We invented paper craft!

Wasps' nest

Vespula vulgaris

BUG BOX

COMMON NAME Common Wasp
SCIENTIFIC NAME *Vespula vulgaris*
FAMILY Vespidae
ORDER Hymenoptera
CLASS Insecta
PHYLUM Arthropoda
KINGDOM Animalia

ADULTS

SIZE 20–25mm
FAVOURITE FOOD Sugary foods and meat
LIKE TO BE Almost anywhere
SEE THEM June to October

FACTABULOUS!

✤ Common Wasps are social insects. They live together in large nests that contain a queen and up to several thousand females called workers.

✤ Wasps form their nests from a type of paper that they make by chewing wood and mixing it with their saliva.

✤ We humans use paper thanks to an observant Chinese man who lived nearly 2,000 years ago. This man watched how wasps made the papery material for their nests, and decided to copy them!

Brown Mayfly

Fitz

Who is pressed for time

Twenty-four hours
Is all I've got
This time tomorrow
That's my lot

The whole of a life
To pack into *one* day
Excuse me now
Must be on my way

I'm in need of a river
In need of a wife
Without them there won't be
A point to my life

I've no time to linger
No time for food
No time to natter
I'm not in the mood

Just show me the water
Beck, river or stream
So I can fulfil
My lifetime's dream

If I mate, leave a legacy
I'll not complain
My life will not have been
Lived in vain.

Ephemera vulgata

BUG BOX

COMMON NAME	Brown Mayfly
SCIENTIFIC NAME	*Ephemera vulgata*
FAMILY	Ephemeridae
ORDER	Ephemeroptera
CLASS	Insecta
PHYLUM	Arthropoda
KINGDOM	Animalia

ADULTS

SIZE	12–20mm
FAVOURITE FOOD	Nothing!
LIKE TO BE	Near still or slow-moving rivers, canals, streams, etc.
SEE THEM	May to September

FACTABULOUS!

- Brown Mayflies spend most of their lives (up to two years) as larvae living in water, where they eat algae and other small creatures.

- Adult mayflies live out of the water – for just one day.

- Adult mayflies have no mouthparts, so they can't eat anything!

- Mayflies get their scientific name from the Greek *ephemeros*, which means 'short-lived'.

Honeybee

Floella

Foraging free

I like to go out when it's sunny
And gather ingredients for honey

My sisters aren't old enough yet
So they play with their geometry set

Holed up indoors, they wax lyrical
The results? Nothing short of a miracle!

Honeybees in their hive

Apis mellifera

BUG BOX

COMMON NAME Honeybee
SCIENTIFIC NAME *Apis mellifera*
FAMILY Apidae
ORDER Hymenoptera
CLASS Insecta
PHYLUM Arthropoda
KINGDOM Animalia

ADULTS

SIZE 12mm
FAVOURITE FOOD Nectar from flowers
LIKE TO BE Near flowers
SEE THEM February to October

FACTABULOUS!

- Honeybees live in a colony that has one queen bee and up to 80,000 worker bees. All the worker bees are the queen's daughters.

- Young worker Honeybees stay in their hive and create wax honeycombs into which the queen lays her eggs.

- Older worker Honeybees go outside and look for pollen (to feed their larvae) and nectar.

- The worker Honeybees collect pollen in baskets on their back legs, just like bumblebees do (see page 12). Can you see the pollen basket in this photo?

- Honeybees produce the honey we like to eat from the nectar they collect.

Leaf-cutter bee

Tin Pan Ali

Belly Dancer

Tummy wiggle, tummy jiggle
Kinked in the air

Pollen shovel, pollen shift
So debonair

Yellower and yellower
Shimmy, shovel, quit

The sweet pea shuffle
Is this summer's hit!

Megachile species

COMMON NAME Leaf-cutter bee
GENUS *Megachile*
FAMILY Megachilidae
ORDER Hymenoptera
CLASS Insecta
PHYLUM Arthropoda
KINGDOM Animalia

ADULTS

SIZE 10–15mm
FAVOURITE FOOD Nectar and pollen
LIKE TO BE In gardens
SEE THEM May to August

FACTABULOUS!

✣ Unlike Honeybees (see page 24) and bumblebees (page 12), leaf-cutter bees don't have pollen baskets on their legs that they can collect pollen in.

✣ Instead, leaf-cutter bees collect pollen on the hairs on their abdomen (their tummy)!

✣ Unlike Honeybees and bumblebees that live in big colonies, leaf-cutter bees are solitary bees. They live on their own.

✣ Leaf-cutter bees get their name from the fact that they cut circles out of leaves, then roll them up to make their nest.

buzz**ing**

à GO-GO!

Millipede

Tillie

Who has lots and lots and lots of legs

I've never managed to count them all
I know there's lots and I know they're small
Without them I couldn't shimmy and crawl
But how many I've got, I don't know.

How many I've got, I haven't a clue
It's definitely more than *you*
You've got a measly total of two
That's not very many at all.

That's not very many, and you can't coil
Yourself up in a spiral so as to foil
Attacks from your enemies scouring the soil
That's more than you can do.

That's more than you can do at all
You're too bony, you're too tall
Try to do it and you'd just fall
Flat on your nose to toe

SPLAT!

Cylindroiulus londinensis

BUG BOX

COMMON NAME	Millipede
SCIENTIFIC NAME	*Cylindroiulus londinensis*
FAMILY	Julidae
ORDER	Julida
CLASS	Diplopoda
PHYLUM	Arthropoda
KINGDOM	Animalia

ADULTS

SIZE	20–48mm
FAVOURITE FOOD	Soft or decaying plants
LIKE TO BE	On the ground, and in compost bins
SEE THEM	At night

FACTABULOUS!

✤ Insects have six legs. Millipedes have lots more than six legs, so they are definitely not insects!

✤ The name Millipede comes from Latin and means 'one thousand legs'. But Millipedes don't really have that many legs.

✤ When they are young, Millipedes only have a few pairs of legs. As they grow they add more segments to their body.

✤ Each body segment has two pairs of legs attached.

✤ So the older a Millipede is, the more legs it has!

✤ Millipedes can coil up into a tight spiral to protect themselves if they are attacked.

31

Common Plume Moth

Emmelina

More than meets the eye

Twiggly twoggly
Miss Emmelina is
Spending her day on my
Window, I see.

Spindly wings outstretched
How she can fly is a
Monodactylian
Mystery to me.

Emmelina monodactyla

BUG BOX

COMMON NAME Common Plume Moth
SCIENTIFIC NAME *Emmelina monodactyla*
FAMILY Pterophoridae
ORDER Lepidoptera
CLASS Insecta
PHYLUM Arthropoda
KINGDOM Animalia

ADULTS

SIZE 18–27mm (wingspan)
FAVOURITE FOOD Nectar from flowers
LIKE TO BE All over the place – especially in hedges
SEE THEM All year round – especially March to November

FACTABULOUS!

⇨ Like all plume moths, the Common Plume Moth's wings are actually made up of things that look a bit like feathers.

⇨ When this moth isn't flying, its feathery wings are rolled up tightly, and look like single fingers.

⇨ The name *monodactyla* comes from the Greek, and means 'single finger'.

⇨ This poem is a special type of poem called a double dactyl. It may be the world's first ever double dactyl about a monodactyl!

European Crane Fly

Cecilia

Who craves more

Not a hectic day today
Time to sunbathe
Time to stay
A little while upon this leaf
And ponder why my life's so brief ...

My legs are long
My life is short
And so it all
Amounts to nought.

Not a lot to do today
Time to sit back
Time to stay
And think about the things that matter
How soon this mortal coil will shatter ...

Oh how I wish
That I could trade
My gangly limbs
For ripe old age.

Not a frantic day today
Time to lounge
Time to stay
Here for a while and cogitate
On why I'm in this parlous state ...

Oh how much better
Life would be
With short legs and
Longevity.

Tipula paludosa

BUG BOX

COMMON NAME	European Crane Fly
SCIENTIFIC NAME	*Tipula paludosa*
FAMILY	Tipulidae
ORDER	Diptera
CLASS	Insecta
PHYLUM	Arthropoda
KINGDOM	Animalia

ADULTS

SIZE	16mm
FAVOURITE FOOD	Not very interested in food at all!
LIKE TO BE	In fields, parks and gardens – and often in houses at the end of summer and beginning of autumn
SEE THEM	May to November, but mostly mid-August to mid-September

FACTABULOUS!

- The European Crane Fly is better known to most of us as the Daddy Longlegs – for obvious reasons!

- Adult crane flies only live for about 10–15 days.

Red-tailed Bumblebee

Kirsty

Queen bee

I'm property hunting this morning
The early bird and all that
I need a hole that's comfy and dry
I've got all my requirements off pat.

I'm property hunting this morning
I've got quite a few sites to view
Location! Location! Location!
Only the best will do.

I'm property hunting this morning
I'll turn it into an HMO
My rapidly expanding family
Will need plenty of room to grow.

I'm property hunting this morning
The decision will be up to me
It's me who wears the trousers
I'm the boss, the top dog, the Queen bee.

Bombus lapidarius

BUG BOX

COMMON NAME Red-tailed Bumblebee (queen)
SCIENTIFIC NAME *Bombus lapidarius*
FAMILY Apidae
ORDER Hymenoptera
CLASS Insecta
PHYLUM Arthropoda
KINGDOM Animalia

ADULTS

SIZE 25mm
FAVOURITE FOOD Nectar and pollen from flowers
LIKE TO BE Near flowers
SEE THEM March to October

FACTABULOUS!

- Queen bumblebees are the only bumblebees that survive the winter. All the worker and male bumblebees die.

- Worker Honeybees, by contrast, *do* survive the winter, by clustering together and eating honey.

- Queen bumblebees survive the winter by hibernating.

- In spring, queen bumblebees wake up from their hibernation and each one goes looking for somewhere to make her nest, and start a new colony.

Common Froghopper

Fred

A potted biog.

The froghopper hops
From June to September
With frequent stops
The froghopper hops
Until he flops
By mid-November
The froghopper hops
From June to September.

Philaenus spumarius

FACTABULOUS!

➥ The Common Froghopper is a champion jumper. It can jump 100 times its own body length!

➥ Some people call froghoppers 'spittle bugs', because young froghoppers (nymphs) develop in a frothy blob that looks like spit. (It's often called 'cuckoo spit'.) You can see this in the photo opposite.

➥ The froghopper nymphs make the froth by blowing air into a liquid that comes out of their bottom!

➥ Look out for cuckoo spit on plants in spring.

Painted Lady

Marilyn

Some like it hot

I'm a Painted Lady
I don't like it shady
I have to feel heat on my wings
My life was begun
Under African sun
Where daily the muezzin sings.

To Britain I've flown
(I say flown, partly blown)
On a journey of mile after mile
And when I wet my whistle
On a fresh northern thistle
I know the long haul was worthwhile.

Though your nectar is sweet
And the views hard to beat
All too soon, I'll say my good-byes
As the leaves start to turn
I'll yearn to burn
Once again under African skies.

Vanessa cardui

BUG BOX

COMMON NAME	Painted Lady
SCIENTIFIC NAME	*Vanessa cardui*
FAMILY	Nymphalidae
ORDER	Lepidoptera
CLASS	Insecta
PHYLUM	Arthropoda
KINGDOM	Animalia

ADULTS

SIZE	64mm (wingspan)
FAVOURITE FOOD	Nectar from thistles and buddleia
LIKE TO BE	Near thistles and/or buddleia
SEE THEM	April to October

FACTABULOUS!

✣ Painted Ladies fly to Britain on a journey of thousands of kilometres, all the way from North Africa.

✣ These butterflies can't survive the winter here, so some return south in the autumn.

✣ Some years we have millions of Painted Ladies in Britain. Other years, hardly any at all.

Silver Y

Wyman

Does what it says on the tin

Why Y?
Well, well
Dear fellow

Why Y?
Why look
Old thing

The answer
Is very
Clearly

Marked
Upon
My wing.

No flies
On me
Dear fellow

No flies
On me
Old thing

Just Ys
On me
Dear fellow

One
Upon
Each wing.

Autographa gamma

COMMON NAME	Silver Y
SCIENTIFIC NAME	*Autographa gamma*
FAMILY	Noctuidae
ORDER	Lepidoptera
CLASS	Insecta
PHYLUM	Arthropoda
KINGDOM	Animalia

ADULTS

SIZE	35–40mm (wingspan)
FAVOURITE FOOD	Nectar
LIKE TO BE	Near flowers
SEE THEM	March to October, in the daytime and at night

FACTABULOUS!

✣ Silver Ys are moths.

✣ Like Painted Lady butterflies (see page 40), Silver Ys fly over to Britain from a long way away. They come here in the spring and autumn from continental Europe.

✣ Silver Ys come in a variety of different colours, from grey to purply black, but they (nearly) always have one silvery 'Y' on each side of their wings.

Fire Bugs

Fire Bugs

*Who know what they like,
and like what they know*

Devon is the only place to be
FIRE FIRE!
It nestles nice and closely to the sea
FIRE FIRE!
It's also got some moor
Which we might go and explore
Yes, Devon is the only place to be.
FIRE FIRE!

Devon is the only place for us
FIRE FIRE!
We live here without bother, without fuss
FIRE FIRE!
There's mallow here a-plenty
So we're always full not empty
Yes, Devon is the only place for us.
FIRE FIRE!

Our cousins on the continent agree
FIRE FIRE!
Britain's not a place they'd want to be
FIRE FIRE!
Except of course for Devon
Next best thing to Fire Bug heaven
Yes, our cousins on the continent agree.
FIRE FIRE!

So, Devon's where we'll live out all our days
FIRE FIRE!
It suits us in so many special ways
FIRE FIRE!
From Land's End to John O'Groats
There's just one place that gets our votes
Yes, it's Devon, Devon, Devon all our days!
FIRE FIRE!

Pyrrhocoris apterus

BUG BOX

COMMON NAME Fire Bug
SCIENTIFIC NAME *Pyrrhocoris apterus*
FAMILY Pyrrhocoridae
ORDER Hemiptera
CLASS Insecta
PHYLUM Arthropoda
KINGDOM Animalia

ADULTS

SIZE 8–12mm
FAVOURITE FOOD Tree Mallow
LIKE TO BE In Devon!
SEE THEM March to November (if you're in Devon)

FACTABULOUS!

✪ I took nearly all the photos in this book in and around my garden in York. But not this photo.

✪ The only known permanent colony of Fire Bugs in Britain is in the south, near Torquay in Devon. That's a long way from my garden up in North Yorkshire.

buzzing

beautiful!

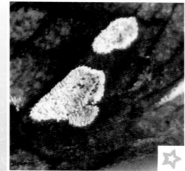

Mint Moth

Cora

A moth of distinction

Yes, I'm crimson and gold – but not common
In fact, I'm rather refined
My markings are subtle and stylish
A cut above average moth-kind.

My antennae too are superior
Look how they're deftly inclined
Their elegance, length and proportions
Leave others trailing behind.

The matter is settled. I think you'll agree
That, as I have just outlined,
I am, it is indisputable,
An uncommonly *special* find.

Pyrausta aurata

BUG BOX

COMMON NAME Mint Moth
SCIENTIFIC NAME *Pyrausta aurata*
FAMILY Crambidae
ORDER Lepidoptera
CLASS Insecta
PHYLUM Arthropoda
KINGDOM Animalia

ADULTS

SIZE 16–20mm (wingspan)
FAVOURITE FOOD Mint and marjoram
LIKE TO BE On mint and marjoram
SEE THEM April to September, in the daytime and at night

FACTABULOUS!

- There are about 2,500 different species of moth in Britain. Some look very similar to each other.

- The Mint Moth, for example, looks very similar to the Common Crimson-and-gold Moth.

- Telling these two moths apart is quite tricky. 'The principal distinguishing feature is the arrangement of the postmedian markings on the forewing'!

Gold Spot

Portia

Precious

All that glisters
Is not gold
But *I* am
I am

Never bought
Never sold
I am
I am

Nature's treasure
Uncontrolled
I am
I am

In your garden
Gold! Behold!
I am
I am.

Plusia festucae

BUG BOX

COMMON NAME Gold Spot
SCIENTIFIC NAME *Plusia festucae*
FAMILY Noctuidae
ORDER Lepidoptera
CLASS Insecta
PHYLUM Arthropoda
KINGDOM Animalia

ADULTS

SIZE 34–46mm
FAVOURITE FOOD Nectar from flowers
LIKE TO BE Near flowers, especially in damp places
SEE THEM June to September

FACTABULOUS!

⇒ The Gold Spot is a moth.

⇒ The gold spots on a Gold Spot's wings aren't really made of gold. But they do glisten just like gold.

⇒ Moth (and butterfly) wings are covered in tiny overlapping scales that have very special properties. When light hits these scales, different colours are produced, including this fabulous metallic gold.

⇒ 'All that glisters is not gold' is a famous quote from a play by William Shakespeare – *The Merchant of Venice*.

Strawberry Snail

Gail

A gastropod with gyratory proclivities

Gail Snail has a fringe and a tail
And a swirling spiral shell
Inside she might have settees and TVs
From the outside no-one can tell.

Gail Snail likes to boogie and flail
She's a performance artist in slime
No need for music, she pumps out a beat
And whirls and jives in time.

Gail Snail leaves a sticky wet trail
In her wake wherever she goes
And if you pad out in your garden tonight
You'll get it all over your toes!

Trochulus striolatus

BUG BOX

COMMON NAME	Strawberry Snail
SCIENTIFIC NAME	*Trochulus striolatus*
FAMILY	Hygromiidae
ORDER	Stylommatophora
CLASS	Gastropoda
PHYLUM	Mollusca
KINGDOM	Animalia

ADULTS

SIZE Shell more than 12mm wide

FAVOURITE FOOD Plants near the ground, especially strawberries

LIKE TO BE Outdoors, in gardens, woods, waste ground ...

SEE THEM Mostly at night, but in the daytime too, after it's rained

FACTABULOUS!

- Snails produce a sticky slime when they move.

- The slime helps them to stick to surfaces and to crawl over obstacles.

- Snails are hermaphrodite. This means they are both male and female.

- So Gail is actually a she *and* a he!

Grass Moth

Parker
And his fireman's hose

My nose is enormous
My hooter is huge
My schnozzle's colossal
The length of a luge

Sticky beak, sticky beak
Easy as pie
Nasal ginormity
Not a clue why.

Agriphila tristella

BUG BOX

COMMON NAME Grass Moth
SCIENTIFIC NAME *Agriphila tristella*
FAMILY Crambidae
ORDER Lepidoptera
CLASS Insecta
PHYLUM Arthropoda
KINGDOM Animalia

ADULTS

SIZE 27mm (wingspan)
FAVOURITE FOOD Nectar from flowers
LIKE TO BE In grassy places – including your lawn!
SEE THEM June to September

FACTABULOUS!

✤ Grass Moths fly at night, and cling to grass stems in the daytime. So look out for them on your lawn or playing field ...

✤ What looks like the moth's nose is actually its 'palps'.

✤ Palps are little feelers that some moths taste with, and others hear with.

55

Common Blue Damselfly

Odette

Out of the blue

Hawkers patrol
Up and down
But ...
I wait wide-eyed
With my wings tight shut.

Darters dart
In and out
But ...
I wait wide-eyed
With my wings tight shut.

Chasers chase
To and fro
But ...
I wait wide-eyed
With my wings tight shut.

Skimmers skim
Side to side
But ...
I wait wide-eyed
With my wings tight shut.

Every now and then
I flounce and flutter
But ...
I'd rather wait wide-eyed
With my wings tight shut.

Hawker Dragonfly

56

Enallagma cyathigerum

BUG BOX

COMMON NAME	Common Blue Damselfly
SCIENTIFIC NAME	*Enallagma cyathigerum*
FAMILY	Coenagrionidae
ORDER	Odonata
CLASS	Insecta
PHYLUM	Arthropoda
KINGDOM	Animalia

ADULTS

SIZE	32–35mm
FAVOURITE FOOD	Flying insects
LIKE TO BE	By large ponds, lakes and rivers
SEE THEM	May to September

FACTABULOUS!

✤ This is a *female* Common Blue Damselfly. Some female Common Blue Damselflies are blue. Some, like this one, aren't.

✤ People sometimes confuse damselflies with dragonflies. But, as you'll see, they are easy to tell apart.

✤ Dragonflies (such as hawkers, darters, chasers and skimmers) hold their wings open when they are at rest. Damselflies hold their wings shut over their back.

✤ Dragonfly eyes are very big, and cover most of their head. Damselfly eyes are smaller, with one at each end of their oblong head.

✤ Dragonflies fly fast and can be very acrobatic. Damselflies can't fly particularly well, and spend more time at rest.

Tawny Mining Bee

The Lone Miner

For whom one is enough

I'm a small bee, a little bee
A solitary mining bee
I don't have many friends
But I don't care
I just saunter round your garden
On my business, now please pardon
Me, I'd like to try that flower
Over there.

I'm a small bee, a little bee
A furry Tawny Mining Bee
I don't go in for monarchies
Or hives
I'm quite happy on my own
Have no desire to be a drone
Or worker bee caught up in other
Apis lives.

I'm a small bee, a little bee
Big on self-sufficiency
A trait all of my progeny
Will share
I dig a nest hole now and then
But I'm not bothered about when
My offspring hatch – what they do next
Is their affair.

Andrena fulva

BUG BOX

COMMON NAME Tawny Mining Bee
SCIENTIFIC NAME *Andrena fulva*
FAMILY Andrenidae
ORDER Hymenoptera
CLASS Insecta
PHYLUM Arthropoda
KINGDOM Animalia

ADULTS

SIZE 8–12mm
FAVOURITE FOOD Nectar from flowers
LIKE TO BE In parks, gardens, woods and grasslands
SEE THEM March to May

FACTABULOUS!

✻ The Tawny Mining Bee is a solitary bee. Unlike social bumblebees and Honeybees, it doesn't live in a big family.

✻ Look out on the ground in springtime for a little mound of soil shaped like a volcano, with a hole in the top. This could be the nest of a Tawny Mining Bee!

✻ A Tawny Mining Bee nest is 20–30cm deep, and has several small holes (called 'brood cells') branching off it.

✻ The female fills each hole with a mixture of nectar and pollen, and then lays one egg there.

✻ When the eggs hatch, the larvae feed on the nectar and pollen that their mother left there for them.

Red velvet mite

Scarlett

Who is very red

If you've got it, flaunt it!
This is my cry
Why be demure?
Why be shy?

A body like mine
Stands out from the crowd
I've every right
To be loud and proud!

Proud to be teency
Proud to be red
Proud to be bouncy
Proud and incred-

ibly vibrant and velvety
Blatant and bold
And I'll stay that way
Till I'm wrinkly and old.

Trombidium species

BUG BOX

COMMON NAME Red velvet mite
GENUS *Trombidium*
FAMILY Trombidiidae
ORDER Trombidiformes
CLASS Arachnida
PHYLUM Arthropoda
KINGDOM Animalia

ADULTS

SIZE 1–5mm
FAVOURITE FOOD Other mites and insects
LIKE TO BE At ground level, especially among dead leaves in woods and forests
SEE THEM April to October

FACTABULOUS!

✤ Mites are tiny! They are the smallest creatures in this book. But red velvet mites are fairly easy to spot because of their bright colour.

✤ A red velvet mite's body is covered in a coat of fine hairs that creates a velvety look.

✤ Adult mites have eight legs and so, like spiders, they are arachnids, not insects.

✤ As you can see in this photo, red velvet mites use their front two legs as antennae.

✤ Scientists believe there may be thousands of different species of red velvet mite, many of them looking very similar. Which is why I can't tell you exactly which species this one is ...

Common Wainscot Moth

Dickie Wainscot

Who's contented

Dickie Wainscot's the name
How do you like my lion's mane?
Don't be scared, I'm quite tame
   Don't you know.
I don't prowl the savannah
For quadruped ani-
mals, I just sit by your lounge window pane.

I'm not head of a pride
Don't have cubs by my side
My horizons aren't wide
   But hey ho.
At night I'm abroad
Completely ignored
But I take all that in my stride.

Wainscot's the name
I'm just a moth, but all the same
I have my place in the game
   Of life.
I'm pleased with my lot
My lot's what I've got
Who needs King of the Jungle fame?

Mythimna pallens

BUG BOX

COMMON NAME	Common Wainscot Moth
SCIENTIFIC NAME	*Mythimna pallens*
FAMILY	Noctuidae
ORDER	Lepidoptera
CLASS	Insecta
PHYLUM	Arthropoda
KINGDOM	Animalia

ADULTS

SIZE	32–40mm
FAVOURITE FOOD	Nectar from flowers
LIKE TO BE	In grassy places, including parks and gardens
SEE THEM	May to October

FACTABULOUS!

✦ There are lots of different Wainscot moths in Britain, including the Obscure Wainscot, Smoky Wainscot and Mathew's Wainscot.

✦ Wainscot moths all belong to the Noctuid moth family, which is the largest of all the moth families. Other Noctuids include the Silver Y (page 42) and the Gold Spot (page 50).

✦ Although moths don't hunt animals, in some tropical parts of the world, male Noctuid moths do feed on the wounds, blood and tear drops of large mammals – including humans!

buzzing hungry!

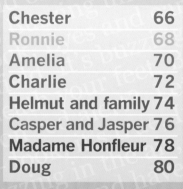

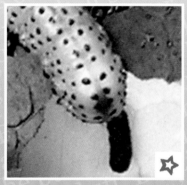

Ruby Tiger Moth caterpillar

Chester

Who likes chomping

Chomping's champion
Chomping's great
Leaves and leaves and
Leaves to be ate

Chomping's champion
Chomping's brill
So many leaves
Such a thrill

Chomping's champion
Chomping's ace
Leaves galore
Stuff my face

Chomping's champion
Can't go wrong
All these leaves!
All day long!

Chomping mini-break
Chomping halt
Take time off
To have a moult

Then back to chomping
Back to chomp
My chlorophyllic
Gastro-romp

Chomping's champion
Chomping's cool
Leaves and leaves and
Leaves as a rule

Chomping's champion
Chomping's fab
Pile on the milligrams
Pile on the flab

Chomping chomping
Till one day
I go to sleep ...
Then fly away.

Phragmatobia fuliginosa

BUG BOX

COMMON NAME	Ruby Tiger Moth (caterpillar)
SCIENTIFIC NAME	*Phragmatobia fuliginosa*
FAMILY	Arctiidae
ORDER	Lepidoptera
CLASS	Insecta
PHYLUM	Arthropoda
KINGDOM	Animalia

CATERPILLARS

SIZE	Up to 35mm
FAVOURITE FOOD	Leaves
LIKE TO BE	On leaves
SEE THEM	Summer and autumn

FACTABULOUS!

✣ Caterpillars have been called eating machines. They eat and eat, and grow and grow.

✣ As they grow, they get too big for their skin, so they moult. When they moult, they shed their skin and grow into a new, bigger one. They generally do this four times.

✣ Caterpillars eat so much because they need enough nutrients to transform into full-sized adult moths (or butterflies) whilst they are pupating.

✣ During pupation, the Ruby Tiger Moth caterpillar transforms into an adult moth that is brick red.

Rosemary Beetle

Ronnie

Veni, vidi, vici

I heard it on the grapevine
York's the place to be
A tourist destination
Higher ranking than Paris!

I heard it on the grapevine
This I gotta see
Medieval walls, a Minster
Sounds like just the place for me!

I heard it on the grapevine
Hitched a ride for free
The journey north was thrilling
Though just a tad chilly!

I heard it on the grapevine
Arrived in time for tea
Fragrant leaves of lavender
And sage and rosemary!

Hey, this York is one hip city
Full of art and bonhomie
I dig it here so much
I think I'll found a colony!

Chrysolina americana

BUG BOX

COMMON NAME	Rosemary Beetle
SCIENTIFIC NAME	*Chrysolina americana*
FAMILY	Chrysomelidae
ORDER	Coleoptera
CLASS	Insecta
PHYLUM	Arthropoda
KINGDOM	Animalia

ADULTS

SIZE	6–7mm
FAVOURITE FOOD	Rosemary, sage and lavender
LIKE TO BE	On rosemary, sage and lavender
SEE THEM	February to October

FACTABULOUS!

⇨ Rosemary Beetles were first discovered in Britain in 1994.

⇨ From their scientific name, *Chrysolina americana*, you might think that they came here from America. They didn't. They came here from southern Europe.

⇨ Rosemary Beetles were first recorded in my home town, York, in 2008. They clearly liked it here, as by 2010 I was seeing lots of them.

⇨ Have you got Rosemary Beetles near you? Have a good look on rosemary, sage, lavender and thyme plants.

⇨ If you find any, tell the Royal Horticultural Society! (See 'Over to You' on page 158.)

⇨ *Veni, vidi, vici* is a famous Latin quote that means 'I came, I saw, I conquered'.

Light Emerald Moth

Amelia
Whose table manners fell short

A Light Emerald Moth from York

Ate with neither a knife nor a fork

She just stuck out her tongue

And sucked as she clung

To a leaf with a grip like a hawk.

Campaea margaritata

BUG BOX

COMMON NAME Light Emerald Moth
SCIENTIFIC NAME *Campaea margaritata*
FAMILY Geometridae
ORDER Lepidoptera
CLASS Insecta
PHYLUM Arthropoda
KINGDOM Animalia

ADULTS

SIZE 30–40mm
FAVOURITE FOOD Nectar from flowers
LIKE TO BE Around deciduous trees, like chestnut, beech and oak
SEE THEM June to September

FACTABULOUS!

✣ There are quite a few Emerald moths, and it can be difficult to tell them apart.

✣ At first I thought this was a Small Emerald Moth.

✣ But when I looked very closely, I saw that it had a tiny red dot at the apex (the tip) of each forewing. This means it's a Light Emerald Moth.

Common Earthworm

Charlie

An earthworm

Charlie is an earthworm, an earthworm, an earthworm
Charlie is an earthworm
He's long and thin and round.

Charlie is an earthworm, an earthworm, an earthworm
Charlie is an earthworm
He lives in the ground.

Charlie's just an earthworm, an earthworm, an earthworm
Charlie's just an earthworm
He's not world renowned.

Charlie is an earthworm, an earthworm, an earthworm
Charlie is an earthworm
Who's just been found.

Charlie *was* an earthworm, an earthworm, an earthworm
Charlie was an earthworm
But ... he's just been eaten by a Blackbird.

Rest In Peace, Charlie.

Lumbricus terrestris

BUG BOX

COMMON NAME	Common Earthworm (Lob Worm)
SCIENTIFIC NAME	*Lumbricus terrestris*
FAMILY	Lumbricidae
ORDER	Haplotaxida
CLASS	Clitellata
PHYLUM	Annelida
KINGDOM	Animalia

ADULTS

SIZE	90–250mm
FAVOURITE FOOD	Dead leaves
LIKE TO BE	In the soil
SEE THEM	When you're digging the soil, or at night

FACTABULOUS!

✣ The Common Earthworm is the largest British earthworm.

✣ The great 19th-century naturalist Charles Darwin discovered that earthworms are some of the most important creatures on planet earth. Why? Because they help make the soil. Without the soil, there would be no plants, and no us!

✣ Darwin realised that 'long before [man] existed, the land was regularly ploughed, and still continues to be thus ploughed by earth-worms.'

✣ Earthworms come up out of the soil at night to pull fallen leaves back into their burrows to eat.

✣ Earthworms are actually hermaphrodite. In other words, like snails (see page 52), they are male and female at the same time.

Berberis Sawfly larvae

Helmut and family

Newcomers to North Yorkshire
(Who eat a lot and excrete a lot)

The first law of thermodynamics,
A maxim sage and true,
States that something cannot become nothing,
Hence this Berberis becomes us and our poo.

P.S. This codicil we've added
     Lest there be any misapprehension.
     What you see before you
     Is no caterpillar convention.

     Butterflies we'll never be,
     Nor moths – not Lepidoptera.
     To be sawflies is our destiny
     Of the order Hymenoptera.

Arge berberidis

FACTABULOUS!

⇨ Berberis Sawflies come from Germany and other parts of Europe.

⇨ They started living in the south of England around 2002.

⇨ In 2006 I found some Berberis Sawfly larvae on the Berberis bush in my garden in York. This was a world-first insect discovery for York! Berberis Sawflies had never been recorded so far north in England before.

⇨ At first I thought they were butterfly or moth caterpillars. But they weren't. The Natural History Museum in London helped me to identify them, and also asked me to send them a sample larva for their collection!

⇨ You can find out lots more about my sawfly discovery at my website. Go to www.theBigBuzz.biz and click on the picture of this book.

Mirids

Casper and Jasper

At home chez Miriam

There are myriad mirids in Miriam's garden
If Miriam did but know it
She's hosting a party
For the glitzy glitterati
Lured by the prospect of Moët.

There are myriad mirids in Miriam's garden
But Miriam and guests are oblivious
While they're sipping champagne
We're content to remain
Focused on matters herbivorous.

There are myriad mirids in Miriam's garden
In fact, we've been here since June
It's our kind of place
A floral-filled space
And this is our favourite bloom.

There are myriad mirids in Miriam's garden
We're her biggest fans by far
We sup on her flowers
For hours and hours
But she doesn't know who we are ...

Stenotus binotatus

BUG BOX

COMMON NAME Mirid
SCIENTIFIC NAME *Stenotus binotatus*
FAMILY Miridae
ORDER Hemiptera
CLASS Insecta
PHYLUM Arthropoda
KINGDOM Animalia

ADULTS

SIZE 5–7mm
FAVOURITE FOOD The flowers and seeds of various grasses
LIKE TO BE In rough grassland
SEE THEM June to September

FACTABULOUS!

✣ Mirids are also known as capsids.

✣ There are over 200 different species of mirid in the British Isles.

✣ There are over 10,000 known species of mirid in the world.

Tree Bumblebee

Madame Honfleur

Oh là là!

Look at me closely
And you will see
I am not an ordinary
Bumblebee.

Regardez-moi bien
And you will see
I am a bumblebee
Of ze tree.

My family
Is d'origine française
But now I consider
Myself Anglaise.

I am 'ere in your jardin
For ze première fois
Bringing my own special
Je ne sais quoi.

I don't come to conquer
I just come to share
To pollinate vos fleurs
Wiz my Gallic flair.

I sink l'Angleterre
Is vraiment géniale
'Ere's to a fruitful
Entente cordiale!

Bombus hypnorum

BUG BOX

COMMON NAME	Tree Bumblebee
SCIENTIFIC NAME	*Bombus hypnorum*
FAMILY	Apidae
ORDER	Hymenoptera
CLASS	Insecta
PHYLUM	Arthropoda
KINGDOM	Animalia

ADULTS

SIZE	10–14mm
FAVOURITE FOOD	Nectar from flowers
LIKE TO BE	Near flowers (to feed), and in bird boxes or holes in trees (to nest)
SEE THEM	March to September

FACTABULOUS!

- Some bumblebees can be a little tricky to identify. But this one is easy. If you see a bumblebee with a white tail and a gingery brown thorax, it's a Tree Bumblebee!
- Tree Bumblebees only arrived in Britain in 2001. They came here from France.
- They were first recorded in my home town of York in 2009. I first saw them in my garden in 2010.
- Have you seen any Tree Bumblebees where you are? If so, let the Bumblebee Conservation Trust know. (See 'Over to You' on page 158.)

Large Black Slug

Doug

Whose tale is easily told

I'm ugly, I'm sticky, I'm slimy, I'm black

I've got a big hole in the side of my back

I'm podgy and squidgy and flabbily fat

And I'll eat all your lettuces – simple as that.

Arion ater

FACTABULOUS!

✤ This Large Black Slug is black. However, Large Black Slugs can also be chestnut brown or orange or pale grey or even creamy white!

✤ Slugs are covered in slimy mucus to stop them drying out.

buzzing
creepy!

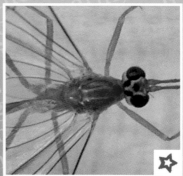

Common Earwig

Errol

A nocturnal nibbler

It's eerie in the garden
When the flies have gone to bed
It's eerie in the garden
That's when we come out instead.
Pincers at the ready
Hackling at the rear
Sharp and curved and pointy
To fill our foes with fear!

It's eerie in the garden
When the bees have gone to bed
We come out a-hunting
For a meal alive or dead.
Jaws in working order
Antennae to the fore
If there's food around here
We'll be finding it for sure!

It's eerie in the garden
When the wasps have gone to bed
We come out in wriggles
With our youngsters to be fed.
Fit and fully rested
Hungry for a bite
Your garden is our snack bar
Where we'll fast-food feast tonight!

Forficula auricularia

BUG BOX

COMMON NAME	Common Earwig
SCIENTIFIC NAME	*Forficula auricularia*
FAMILY	Forficulidae
ORDER	Dermaptera
CLASS	Insecta
PHYLUM	Arthropoda
KINGDOM	Animalia

ADULTS

SIZE	10–15mm
FAVOURITE FOOD	Dead plants, but also flowers and some insects
LIKE TO BE	Almost anywhere
SEE THEM	At night, mostly in summer (but you might spot them hibernating in winter)

FACTABULOUS!

✣ Most insects lay their eggs then leave and have nothing more to do with them. Earwigs are different. Earwigs look after their eggs, and then look after their young once they have hatched.

✣ Most insect eggs hatch out into larvae that don't look at all like the adult insects. Earwigs are different. Their eggs hatch out into nymphs that look the same as the adults, only smaller.

✣ Look under a stone or in a crevice in the summer and you might see lots of earwig families – males and females and young.

✣ Male and female earwigs are easy to tell apart: males have very curly pincers; females have straighter pincers.

Cinnabar Moth caterpillar

Sinbad

Toxic

Eat me at your peril
Eat me and bid farewell
To those you love and cherish
I herald your death-knell.

> *My pleasure is your poison*
> *My fancy kills you cold*
> *The toxins I metabolise*
> *Will stop you growing old.*

Ragwort is my fancy
It fills my waking hours
Its foliage so delicate
Its pretty yellow flowers.

> *My pleasure is your poison*
> *My fancy kills you cold*
> *The toxins I metabolise*
> *Will stop you growing old.*

I've given you fair warning
These stripes are hard to miss
My colour-coded message
Quite simply, dears, is this:

> *My pleasure is your poison*
> *My fancy kills you cold*
> *The toxins I metabolise*
> *Will stop you growing old.*

Tyria jacobaeae

BUG BOX

COMMON NAME Cinnabar Moth (caterpillar)
SCIENTIFIC NAME *Tyria jacobaeae*
FAMILY Arctiidae
ORDER Lepidoptera
CLASS Insecta
PHYLUM Arthropoda
KINGDOM Animalia

CATERPILLARS

SIZE Up to 30mm
FAVOURITE FOOD Ragwort
LIKE TO BE Where there is ragwort (often on waste ground or in fields)
SEE THEM Summer

FACTABULOUS!

⮞ Ragwort is a plant that is poisonous to many animals. For example, it can kill a horse. However, the Cinnabar Moth caterpillar loves it!

⮞ The yellow and black stripes of the Cinnabar Moth caterpillar make it look very unpleasant to eat.

⮞ And it *would* be very unpleasant to eat as it's full of toxins from all the ragwort it's been eating!

⮞ The adult Cinnabar Moth also looks unpleasant to eat. It's not yellow and black, but a striking red and black.

Garden Spider

Ariadne

Who knows her worth

Eight legs are four times better than two
So I am four times better than *you*.
I can make draglines, I can spin webs
I can eat husbands and I can lay eggs.
Yes, eight legs are four times better than two
So I am four times better than *you*.

Eight eyes are four times better than two
So I am four times better than *you*.
I can trap flies when they're in full flight
And make grown ladies flee in fright.
Yes, eight eyes are four times better than two
So I am four times better than *you*.

Araneus diadematus

BUG BOX

COMMON NAME Garden Spider
SCIENTIFIC NAME *Araneus diadematus*
FAMILY Araneidae
ORDER Araneae
CLASS Arachnida
PHYLUM Arthropoda
KINGDOM Animalia

ADULTS

SIZE 6.5–20mm (females)

FAVOURITE FOOD Insects (that fly into their web)

LIKE TO BE In gardens, hedgerows and woods

SEE THEM June to October

FACTABULOUS!

✣ Insects have six legs. Spiders have eight, so they are not insects but arachnids.

✣ Insects have two eyes. Most British spiders have eight.

✣ All spiders produce silk from spinnerets at the end of their body.

✣ Different spiders build silk webs in different shapes. The Garden Spider is an orb weaver. Orb weavers build a sticky web in a spiral shape.

✣ Every few days the Garden Spider eats its web, and then produces a new one.

Zebra Spider

Zac

The attacker

I jump and jab

Grab and nab

Who needs a web?

Not me!

I bungee bounce

Pounce and trounce

I'm a hunter

Wild and free!

Salticus scenicus

BUG BOX

COMMON NAME Zebra Spider
SCIENTIFIC NAME *Salticus scenicus*
FAMILY Salticidae
ORDER Araneae
CLASS Arachnida
PHYLUM Arthropoda
KINGDOM Animalia

ADULTS

SIZE 5–7mm
FAVOURITE FOOD Small insects
LIKE TO BE On sunny walls
SEE THEM April to October

FACTABULOUS!

✄ Not all spiders spin webs. The Zebra Spider is a spider that doesn't spin a web.

✄ The Zebra Spider is a jumping spider. Instead of waiting for prey to fly into a web, the Zebra Spider hunts its prey, and then catches it by jumping on it.

✄ Zebra Spiders can jump up to 10cm!

✄ Like all spiders, the Zebra Spider produces silk. Before it jumps it attaches a bit of silk to a surface as a safety rope, just like a bungee jumper.

Daddy Long-legs Spider

Carys

Who is very protective

I do all the childcare
I look after them night and day
I don't trust nannies
Or au pairs or grannies
And after-school clubs? No way!

I do all the childcare
I look after them day and night
From when they are eggs
To when they've got legs
They'll never be out of my sight.

I do all the childcare
I look after them night and day
They're here in this sac
So I always keep track
Of them – none can go astray.

I do all the childcare
I look after them day and night
They're never in danger
At risk from a stranger
My treasures I hold onto tight.

I've done all the childcare
And soon my darlings will hatch
My organic crèche
Has protected their flesh
From the slightest bruise or scratch.

Pholcus phalangioides

Egg sac

BUG BOX

COMMON NAME	Daddy Long-legs Spider
SCIENTIFIC NAME	*Pholcus phalangioides*
FAMILY	Pholcidae
ORDER	Araneae
CLASS	Arachnida
PHYLUM	Arthropoda
KINGDOM	Animalia

ADULTS

SIZE	Body up to 10mm; legs up to six times longer
FAVOURITE FOOD	Insects and other spiders
LIKE TO BE	Indoors, in houses and other buildings
SEE THEM	All year round

FACTABULOUS!

✤ If you see a tangle of spider silk in your house where the wall meets the ceiling, you may well be looking at a Daddy Long-legs Spider's web.

✤ That's where I saw this Daddy Long-legs Spider in our house.

✤ Female Daddy Long-legs Spiders look after their eggs in a sac made out of their silk. They keep hold of this egg sac with their jaws, as you can see in this photo.

✤ Wolf spiders also carry their eggs around in a silken sac, but they hold their sac at the other end of their body.

Flesh-fly

Kiera

Sure Start

Life's a competition
Life is a race
So skip to the action
Cut to the chase

Don't waste time
As a useless egg
Lay your kids live
Give them a leg-

Up, an instant advantage
Fitter than most
Straightaway ready
To feed on their host

Their meals are all sorted
Local and fresh
Specially selected
Dead animal flesh

Carcasses, carrion
High-protein food
Only the best corpse
Will do for my brood.

Sarcophaga carnaria

BUG BOX

COMMON NAME	Flesh-fly
SCIENTIFIC NAME	*Sarcophaga carnaria*
FAMILY	Sarcophagidae
ORDER	Diptera
CLASS	Insecta
PHYLUM	Arthropoda
KINGDOM	Animalia

ADULTS

SIZE	10–15mm
FAVOURITE FOOD	Nectar from flowers
LIKE TO BE	Most places, often near (but not inside) buildings
SEE THEM	All year round

FACTABULOUS!

- Like spiders, most insects lay eggs. Flesh-flies don't. Flesh-flies are viviparous. That means they give birth to live larvae, rather than laying eggs that later hatch out into larvae.
- Flesh-flies give birth to their larvae on dead animals that the larvae like to eat. That's where they get the name Flesh-fly from.
- *Sarcophaga*, the first word of their scientific name, comes from the Greek *sarco* meaning 'flesh', and *phage* meaning 'eating'.

Black Garden Ants

The Gang

A force to be reckoned with

There's strength in numbers
And numbers in strength
We could explain this
All at great length.

Instead we suggest
You watch us at work
Tiny we may be
But work we don't shirk.

Watch us move corpses
Back to our nest
Watch us on forays
Put to the test.

Discipline! Teamwork!
Divided we fall
One is nothing
Many is all.

Lasius niger

FACTABULOUS!

✣ Like bumblebees and Honeybees, ants are social insects and live in big colonies.

✣ A Black Garden Ant colony can have as many as 15,000 ants!

✣ Ant colonies are very organised. There is a queen which, to begin with, has wings. She lays eggs that turn into smaller, wingless females called workers. In the late spring or summer, some eggs develop into winged males.

✣ Look for ant colonies when you are outdoors, and watch the workers at work.

Yellow Ophion Ichneumon Wasp

Lucretia

Who is explaining the facts of life to some caterpillars

For my babies to live
    You must die
I inject
    In the blink of an eye
My eggs in your tummies
    And then off I fly
For my babies to live
    You must die.

When my eggs hatch
    They'll eat you all up
On your organs
    My babies will sup
They'll hollow you out
    Like a bone china cup
When my eggs hatch
    They'll eat you all up.

Once you're dead you'll just
    Drop off your leaf
Your life, it's true,
    Will be brief
There'll be no crowds of mourners
    Wracked with grief
Once you're dead you'll just
    Drop off your leaf.

But alive you are
    Just what I need
You're a super
    Nutritious feed
For an ichneumon mummy
    You're manna indeed
Yes alive you are
    Just what I need.

Ready? This won't hurt a bit ...

JAB!

Ophion luteus

BUG BOX

COMMON NAME Yellow Ophion Ichneumon Wasp
SCIENTIFIC NAME *Ophion luteus*
FAMILY Ichneumonidae
ORDER Hymenoptera
CLASS Insecta
PHYLUM Arthropoda
KINGDOM Animalia

ADULTS

SIZE 15–20mm
FAVOURITE FOOD Nectar from flowers
LIKE TO BE Places with plenty of flowers, and in houses on summer and autumn evenings
SEE THEM July to October, more often at night

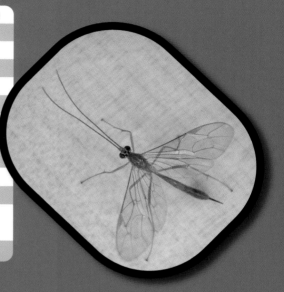

FACTABULOUS!

✿ Ichneumon wasps are parasitoid wasps. This means they lay their eggs in the bodies of live caterpillars, and when the eggs hatch, the larvae eat – and kill – the caterpillars from the inside.

✿ The female Yellow Ophion Ichneumon Wasp lays her eggs in moth caterpillars.

✿ The long needle at the end of her body is called an ovipositor (Latin for 'egg placer').

✿ She uses her ovipositor like a syringe to prick through a caterpillar's skin and inject her eggs.

buzzing

nifty!

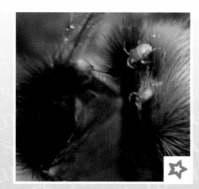

Mites

Steve and his colleagues
Who fly FleasyJet B2B

We're spending some of our air miles
On a short-haul domestic flight
Making a bee-line for ... not quite sure where
No luggage – we're travelling light.

There's no in-flight entertainment
No frills at all, just fur
The view from here is lousy
Things are pretty much of a blur.

The seating's fairly basic too
Just a matter of holding on tight
But hey, it's a total freebie
So's our connecting flight.

Our final destination (we hope)
Is a hive where security's lax
By then we'll be a mite peckish
And head straight for their waxy snacks!

Parasitellus species

BUG BOX

COMMON NAME Mite
GENUS *Parasitellus*
FAMILY Parasitidae
ORDER Mesostigmata
CLASS Arachnida
PHYLUM Arthropoda
KINGDOM Animalia

ADULTS

SIZE 1–2mm
FAVOURITE FOOD Pollen and wax in bumblebees' nests
LIKE TO BE In bumblebees' nests
SEE THEM March to November

FACTABULOUS!

✿ These mites like to eat food they find in bumblebees' nests.

✿ But they can't fly at all, or walk very well. So to get to a new bumblebee's nest, they hitch a ride on the bumblebee that's leaving its nest, hop off when the bee stops on a flower, then hitch a ride on a different bumblebee (in this photo an Early Bumblebee) to its nest.

✿ When a new queen emerges from a nest at the end of the summer, lots of mites hitch a ride on her and stay attached to her all through winter whilst she hibernates.

✿ The mites don't do any harm to the bumblebees – but they can weigh them down a bit!

✿ There are a number of different species of *Parasitellus* mite that hitch rides on bumblebees. From this photo, I can't tell you which species these ones are.

Black Clock Beetle

Archie

A professional assassin

I don't like the limelight
I don't like the glare
Of publicity, cameras,
People who stare.

I prefer undercover work
Scuttling at speed
Hot on the trail
Of a nocturnal feed.

Danger? No problem.
This, you'll have guessed,
Is my very own purpose-built
Bullet-proof vest.

I'm the scourge of the underworld
Tough as they come.
Get in my way
You'll end up in my tum.

Pterostichus madidus

BUG BOX

COMMON NAME	Black Clock Beetle
SCIENTIFIC NAME	*Pterostichus madidus*
FAMILY	Carabidae
ORDER	Coleoptera
CLASS	Insecta
PHYLUM	Arthropoda
KINGDOM	Animalia

ADULTS

SIZE	12–18mm
FAVOURITE FOOD	Caterpillars, slugs and strawberries
LIKE TO BE	In gardens and fields
SEE THEM	All year round

FACTABULOUS!

- The Black Clock Beetle is a ground beetle. (So is the Green Tiger Beetle on page 120.)

- Ground beetles have long legs, so they can run quickly to hunt down their prey.

- The Black Clock Beetle is nocturnal. It spends the day under cover, underneath stones or loose bark or in tussocks of grass.

- Its wing cases are fused together. The downside of this is that it can't fly. The upside is that the wing cases act as tough protective armour.

- The Black Clock Beetle is also known as the Strawberry Beetle, because of its fondness for strawberries.

Sawfly

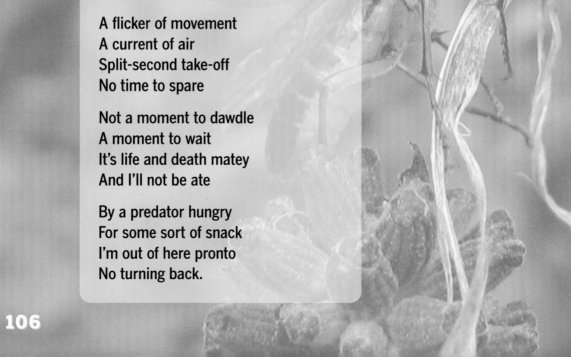

Lara

On a wing and a prayer

My antennae are up
I'm on red alert
At the first sign of danger
I'm off, that's a cert

A flicker of movement
A current of air
Split-second take-off
No time to spare

Not a moment to dawdle
A moment to wait
It's life and death matey
And I'll not be ate

By a predator hungry
For some sort of snack
I'm out of here pronto
No turning back.

Tenthredo mesomela

BUG BOX

COMMON NAME Sawfly
SCIENTIFIC NAME *Tenthredo mesomela*
FAMILY Tenthredinidae
ORDER Hymenoptera
CLASS Insecta
PHYLUM Arthropoda
KINGDOM Animalia

ADULTS

SIZE 10–15mm

FAVOURITE FOOD Nectar and pollen, but also small insects

LIKE TO BE Most places, especially around flowers

SEE THEM May to July

FACTABULOUS!

⇨ Like all insects, sawflies have antennae.

⇨ Insects use their antennae to sense things such as movement, smell and sound.

⇨ Sawflies are called sawflies because the females have a kind of saw at the end of their abdomen.

⇨ They use this saw to cut holes in plants, into which they lay their eggs.

⇨ You can see a video of a sawfly doing just this at my website. Go to www.theBigBuzz.biz and click on the picture of this book.

Hummingbird Hawk-moth

Howard

A brief encounter

It's humming

It's coming

It's supping

It's ... *gone!*

A blur

At a fleur

And a tongue

Then it's ... *gone!*

Flashes of orange

Shimmers of brown

The Hummingbird Hawk-moth

Has been in town.

Macroglossum stellatarum

FACTABULOUS!

- When it's feeding at a flower, the Hummingbird Hawk-moth looks very much like a hummingbird.

- It hovers just above the flower with its wings beating very very fast.

- It has a long tongue that can reach deep into flowers to get to the nectar.

- The Hummingbird Hawk-moth flies during the daytime. So, keep a very beady eye out in the summer, and you might just catch a glimpse of one!

White-lipped Banded Snail

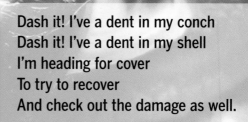

Rufus

Who is rueful

Dash it! I've a dent in my conch
Dash it! I've a dent in my shell
I've just been attacked
And left splintered and cracked
I don't think this bodes very well.

Dash it! I've a dent in my conch
Dash it! I've a dent in my shell
I think I'm in shock
I need to take stock
I'm really not feeling that well.

Dash it! I've a dent in my conch
Dash it! I've a dent in my shell
I'm heading for cover
To try to recover
And check out the damage as well.

Dash it! I've lots of dents in my conch
Dash it! I've lots of dents in my shell
Will they heal? Will I mend?
Or is this the end?
Only time will tell ...

Cepaea hortensis

BUG BOX

COMMON NAME White-lipped Banded Snail
SCIENTIFIC NAME *Cepaea hortensis*
FAMILY Helicidae
ORDER Stylommatophora
CLASS Gastropoda
PHYLUM Mollusca
KINGDOM Animalia

ADULTS

SIZE Shell up to 25mm wide

FAVOURITE FOOD Nettles, ragwort and hogweed

LIKE TO BE In gardens, hedgerows, woodland, fields ...

SEE THEM March to October, especially on damp, mild days

FACTABULOUS!

✪ Snails can survive serious injuries to their shells.

✪ A snail expert told me that he once found a snail that had been trodden on by a cow:

'You've never seen such a mess – yet it had recovered and repaired the shell as best it could.'

Bluebottle

Betty

Who feels unloved

People don't like me
I don't know why
What's so wrong
With being a fly?

Look at my thorax
So shiny and clean
One of the loveliest
You've ever seen!

It's domed and metallic
With bristling black hairs
Why is it nobody
Anywhere cares?

They just want to swat me
Or shoo me away
They never invite me
In to play.

People don't like me
But I like them
And their knives and their forks
And their plates and their stem-

Ware, their fruit and their fridges
Their bowls and their bins
Their jams, their jellies
Their just emptied tins.

People don't like me
That makes me sad
They don't see the *good* in me
Only the bad.

Calliphora vomitoria

BUG BOX

COMMON NAME	Bluebottle
SCIENTIFIC NAME	*Calliphora vomitoria*
FAMILY	Calliphoridae
ORDER	Diptera
CLASS	Insecta
PHYLUM	Arthropoda
KINGDOM	Animalia

ADULTS

SIZE	10–14mm
FAVOURITE FOOD	Meat and other dead or dying material
LIKE TO BE	Almost anywhere
SEE THEM	All year round – but most common in summer

FACTABULOUS!

✣ The word *vomitoria* in the Bluebottle's scientific name is very apt, as Bluebottles regurgitate (vomit up) their food into a bubble. You can see this happening in the photo here.

✣ It's generally only *female* Bluebottles that enter our houses.

✣ They lay their eggs in their food – which is sometimes our food too. This explains why people don't like them! (Would *you* like to eat food that has Bluebottle eggs in it?)

Black-tailed Skimmer

Major Teneral

Odonata air-borne division

The time has come
D-day's here
Landing on the shore
All clear?

Three aquatic years
Have passed
Time to shed
My larval cast.

I've split my skin
Broken free
From bondage cold
And watery.

Pumped and primed
Within the hour
Once I'm dry
I'll have air power!

I'll jink and skim,
Hover, patrol,
Dart, reverse,
Cruise control.

Yes, my metamorphosis
Is incomplete
But in the sky
I'll be hard to beat.

Orthetrum cancellatum

BUG BOX

COMMON NAME	Black-tailed Skimmer
SCIENTIFIC NAME	*Orthetrum cancellatum*
FAMILY	Libellulidae
ORDER	Odonata
CLASS	Insecta
PHYLUM	Arthropoda
KINGDOM	Animalia

ADULTS

SIZE	44–50mm long; 77mm wingspan
FAVOURITE FOOD	Flying insects
LIKE TO BE	Near fresh water, especially lakes
SEE THEM	May to September

FACTABULOUS!

- Dragonflies live most of their life in water as larvae, called nymphs.
- Then, after several years, they come up on land, break out of their larval 'cast' (as you can see happening in the photo opposite) and emerge as adult dragonflies.
- This is called incomplete metamorphosis, and it's quite unusual. Most insects undergo *complete* metamorphosis, which includes an inbetween stage (called pupation) before they become adults. (See page 132.)
- When dragonflies first emerge from their larval cast, they are called tenerals.
- Dragonflies fly very fast – up to 54km per hour – and they are very agile.
- Adult dragonflies only live for about eight weeks.

Common Field Grasshopper

Jack

Who is hopping glad

'There's a cricket in the thicket
Just the ticket! Think I'll pick it
Up and take it home and show it
To my Dad.'

*'Sticky wicket! I must hop it
I won't stick around and cop it
Think you'd really better stop it
Little lad.'*

B O I N G !

*'And by the way, you've come a cropper
Not a cricket, a grasshopper
My antennae aren't so whopper
Look it up.'*

B O I N G !

*'I'm all-round neater, sing much sweeter
Not a night owl, or meat eater
And I like to think I'm fleeter
Little pup.'*

B O I N G !

'Where's it gone? It was here
It can't just disappear
I saw it here just near
This fallen tree.'

*'Well that's no great surprise
I'm a master of disguise
I'm right here before your eyes
Look this is me.'*

B O I N G !

'I give up, I'm going home
It's no fun here all alone
I wonder what there'll be
For tea tonight

Maybe pizza, maybe rice
Or some pasta would be nice
Or my favourite, beans on ...'

B O I N G !

'Arrgh!'
'Gave you a fright?!'

B O I N G !
B O I N G !
B O I N G !

Chorthippus brunneus

BUG BOX

COMMON NAME	Common Field Grasshopper
SCIENTIFIC NAME	*Chorthippus brunneus*
FAMILY	Acrididae
ORDER	Orthoptera
CLASS	Insecta
PHYLUM	Arthropoda
KINGDOM	Animalia

ADULTS

SIZE	15–24mm
FAVOURITE FOOD	Grasses
LIKE TO BE	In short vegetation
SEE THEM	June to October

FACTABULOUS!

✤ Grasshoppers and crickets are both in the same order, Orthoptera (from the Greek *ortho* meaning 'straight', and *ptera*, 'wings'). They are called this because their wings are laid straight back along their bodies.

✤ Grasshoppers and crickets look quite similar, but it's easy to tell them apart.

✤ Grasshoppers have short antennae, whereas crickets have very long ones.

✤ Grasshoppers and crickets can both jump long distances. Grasshoppers can jump about 20 times their body length.

✤ They can jump so far because they have catapults built into their long back legs.

buzzing
green!

Green Tiger Beetle

Tyger

Coleopteral symmetry

Tyger Tyger, burnished bright,
In the forest's dappled light;
What immortal hand unseen,
Did flame thy form metallic green?

What the spray can? What the ink,
Did paint thy legs pearlescent pink?
What dread eyes! And what dread claws!
What brain trained thy deadly jaws?

Tyger Tyger burnished bright,
On the ground, just to my right:
What immortal hand unseen,
Did flame thy form metallic green?

Cicindela campestris

BUG BOX

COMMON NAME Green Tiger Beetle
SCIENTIFIC NAME *Cicindela campestris*
FAMILY Carabidae
ORDER Coleoptera
CLASS Insecta
PHYLUM Arthropoda
KINGDOM Animalia

ADULTS

SIZE 12–15mm
FAVOURITE FOOD Insects and other invertebrates
LIKE TO BE In areas with bare ground
SEE THEM April to October

FACTABULOUS!

✤ The Green Tiger Beetle is one of the few creatures in this book that I have never seen in my garden. I saw this one in a nearby nature reserve.

✤ With its long legs, the Green Tiger Beetle can run fast.

✤ I have based my poem on a famous poem by William Blake called 'The Tyger'. Do you know that poem?

Common Green Lacewing

Philippe

Who is smitten

My love is dainty as a doily
A filigree of light
A flounce of fine-tuned fluttering
A feuilleté of flight.

She is all I ever dreamed of
With eyes of burning gold
And I'm tremulating torridly
To have her and to hold.

Chrysoperla carnea

BUG BOX

COMMON NAME	Common Green Lacewing
SCIENTIFIC NAME	*Chrysoperla carnea*
FAMILY	Chrysopidae
ORDER	Neuroptera
CLASS	Insecta
PHYLUM	Arthropoda
KINGDOM	Animalia

ADULTS

SIZE	15mm
FAVOURITE FOOD	Aphids
LIKE TO BE	In gardens, parks and woods, but quite often indoors too
SEE THEM	May to August, mostly at night

FACTABULOUS!

▷ Lacewings are sometimes known as 'golden-eyes', because of their beautiful golden eyes.

▷ Lacewings court by tremulating. To tremulate, they vibrate their abdomen. This creates a sound that makes whatever they are standing on vibrate too.

▷ Scientists recently discovered that the Common Green Lacewing isn't just one species, but several different species that can only be told apart by the sort of tremulating they do!

Greenbottle

Grania

No contest

I'm a *Green*bottle
Not a Bluebottle

I've a *green* body
Not a blue body

And a *green* botty
Not a blue botty

But we've both got red eyes.

I'm Lucilia
She's Calliphora

I'm much prettier
And I like flora

She's much sillier
And an indoors-er

But we're both called blow-flies.

I'm a *Green*bottle
I'm the *Queen* bottle

I've a *green* body
A *supreme* body

And a *green* botty
Not at *all* spotty

That's why *I* win first prize!

Lucilia caesar

BUG BOX

COMMON NAME Greenbottle
SCIENTIFIC NAME *Lucilia caesar*
FAMILY Calliphoridae
ORDER Diptera
CLASS Insecta
PHYLUM Arthropoda
KINGDOM Animalia

ADULTS

SIZE 8–15mm

FAVOURITE FOOD Pollen and nectar

LIKE TO BE Outdoors, especially where there are flowers

SEE THEM All year, particularly April to October

FACTABULOUS!

✪ Unlike Bluebottles (*Calliphora vomitoria* – see page 112), Greenbottles hardly ever come into our houses.

✪ However, like Bluebottles, Greenbottles lay their eggs on meat and rotting animals.

✪ Meat that has eggs laid on it used to be called 'fly-blown'. Which is where Bluebottles and Greenbottles got their name 'blow-flies' from.

Green Dock Beetle

Jade

Who's expecting

It isn't triplets
It isn't twins
It isn't quads
And it isn't quins.

There's scores and scores
And scores of the things.
So many eggs
I can't close my wings.

All in my tummy
But not for long.
I'll lay them tomorrow
And then I'll be gone.

Gastrophysa viridula

BUG BOX

COMMON NAME	Green Dock Beetle
SCIENTIFIC NAME	*Gastrophysa viridula*
FAMILY	Chrysomelidae
ORDER	Coleoptera
CLASS	Insecta
PHYLUM	Arthropoda
KINGDOM	Animalia

ADULTS

SIZE	4–8mm
FAVOURITE FOOD	Dock leaves
LIKE TO BE	On dock leaves, preferably near water
SEE THEM	March to October

FACTABULOUS!

✼ When she is full of eggs, the female Green Dock Beetle becomes so swollen that her wing cases (her elytra) don't fit properly any more, and they end up perched on the top of her shiny black abdomen – just like in this photo.

✼ A female Green Dock Beetle lives for about 35 days. In that time she can lay over 1,000 eggs.

Sage Leafhopper

Alex

Whose lineage is long

For 125 million years
  My family has roamed planet earth
For 125 million years
  We have been proving our worth
We went forth and multiplied
  Long ago
Now we're a global sensation
  You know
We're leafhoppers, see?
  And where would the world be
Without my aunts and uncles
  And me?

Our family is ... massive
  There's no other word
And if one day
  It ever occurred
To you to count all the mammals
  And reptiles that exist
And to add all the birds
  And amphibs to the list
I think you might be
  Surprised to find
There's many times more
  Of us leafhopper-kind.

There's 20,000 species
  At least
100K maybe
  A veritable feast
Of leafhopper
  Biodiversity
Studied at many a
  University
We sing like cicadas
  We leafhopper rap
And the key to our success
  Is freshly sucked sap.

Eupteryx melissae

FACTABULOUS!

⤷ There are more species of leafhopper in the world than there are species of birds, mammals, reptiles and amphibians put together.

⤷ Leafhoppers feed by sucking the sap from plants, and so they are found almost anywhere there are plants, from tropical rainforests to the Arctic.

⤷ Leafhoppers have been around for a long, long time. The oldest leafhopper fossils are from the Lower Cretaceous period, which was 125 million years ago.

Green Shield Bug

Jean

A seasonal fashionista

There was a young shield bug called Jean

Who spent spring and all summer bright green

Then in autumn, it's said,

She turned deep bronzy red

And through winter she never was seen ...

Palomena prasina

FACTABULOUS!

✪ The Green Shield Bug changes colour in autumn from green to bronzy red, and then it hibernates.

✪ Although shield bugs look a bit like beetles, they're not beetles (in the order Coleoptera) but true bugs (Hemiptera).

✪ All Hemipterans have piercing mouthparts, and so can reach the sap in plants.

✪ Leafhoppers (see page 128) are also members of the order Hemiptera. As are several other insects in this book ...

Green-veined White pupa

Stan

Still

I have suspended my animation
Disguised myself as vegetation
To undergo a transformation
Beyond your wildest imagination.

Weeks of internal reorganisation
Antennal and proboscal generation
Gradual bilateral wing creation
Crucial muscular calibration.

Soon, the moment of revelation
Release from my verdant encapsulation
Into my final incarnation
This is the wonder of pupation.

Pieris napi

BUG BOX

COMMON NAME Green-veined White (pupa)
SCIENTIFIC NAME *Pieris napi*
FAMILY Pieridae
ORDER Lepidoptera
CLASS Insecta
PHYLUM Arthropoda
KINGDOM Animalia

PUPAE

SIZE about 20mm
FAVOURITE FOOD None – they can't feed whilst pupating
LIKE TO BE On plant stems, tree trunks, fences and buildings
SEE THEM Almost all year round

FACTABULOUS!

✹ The Green-veined White is a butterfly.

✹ The life cycle of butterflies (and moths) is: egg, caterpillar, pupa, adult. This is called complete metamorphosis.

✹ To make sure it doesn't fall off the place it's chosen to pupate, the pupa attaches itself with a cremaster (support hooks) and a silk thread called a girdle. Can you see the girdle on this photo?

✹ Adult Green-veined White butterflies look very similar to Small White butterflies. To tell them apart, look at the underside of their wings. The Green-veined White has tell-tale grey-green lines along some of its veins (as you can see in the photo opposite). The Small White butterfly doesn't have these lines.

Tansy Beetle

Gemma

The Jewel of York

'Twas Jorvik, and the chrysomelids
Did shine and shimmer by the Ouse;
All visity were the school kids,
And the pleasure crafts did cruise.

'Watch out for Chrysolina graminis!
The elytra pitted, iridescent green!
The pronotum smooth and, oh what bliss,
The body's coppery sheen!'

She took her digicam in hand:
Long time the sequined gem she sought –
So rested she at Fulford Ings,
And stood awhile in thought.

And as in huffish thought she stood,
The Tansy Beetles, of great fame,
Came squiffling through the tangled weeds,
And nibbled as they came!

One, two! Three, four! And more and more
She shot the creatures, snicker-snap!
With her pix, she got her kicks
Then went home for a nap.

'And hast *thou* seen the Tansy Beetle?
Go walk on the ings, and if beetles be ahoy
Oh tansy day! Coleopteral hurray!
Thou shalt chortle in thy joy.'

'Twas Jorvik, and the chrysomelids
Did shine and shimmer by the Ouse;
All visity were the school kids,
And the pleasure crafts did cruise.

Chrysolina graminis

BUG BOX

COMMON NAME Tansy Beetle

SCIENTIFIC NAME *Chrysolina graminis*

FAMILY Chrysomelidae

ORDER Coleoptera

CLASS Insecta

PHYLUM Arthropoda

KINGDOM Animalia

ADULTS

SIZE 10mm

FAVOURITE FOOD Tansy

LIKE TO BE On tansy plants along the banks of the River Ouse in and around York

SEE THEM April to June, and August to September

FACTABULOUS!

✣ The only place in Britain where you can see this beetle is along the banks of the River Ouse in and around my home town, York (known by the Vikings as Jorvik).

✣ In the sunlight, the Tansy Beetle glistens like an emerald, and so is known as 'The Jewel of York'.

✣ In Victorian times people used to come to York specially to see this beautiful, rare beetle.

✣ Some people say that Victorian ladies used Tansy Beetles' wing cases as sequins to decorate their clothes. Other people tell me I shouldn't believe everything I hear!

✣ Can you recognise the famous poem that I have based 'Gemma' on?

buzzing dotty!

7-spot Ladybird

Lottie

A love story

Lottie, I'm dotty about you!
I think of you night and day
Basking on your marjoram bush
Then pattering on your way ...

Lottie, I'm dotty about you!
I'm dotty about the curve
Of your graceful, arcing silhouette
It fills me with vigour and verve ...

Lottie, I'm dotty about you!
I'm dotty about your spots
Gleaming, symmetrical, beautifully poised
I love them lots and lots ...

Lottie, I'm dotty about you!
Do you feel the same way about me?
Let's elope to the edge of the garden
And make babies under the tree ...

Coccinella septempunctata

FACTABULOUS!

✪ Ladybirds are beetles (in the order Coleoptera).

✪ Like all beetles, their real wings are hidden under their shiny, hard, outer wing cases.

✪ The scientific name for the ladybird family is 'Coccinellidae'. This comes from the Latin word for scarlet.

✪ The word *septempunctata* is Latin for '7-spotted'.

22-spot Ladybird

Thea

Who likes to strut her spots

Red and black
Is so passé
So last year
No cachet
Red and black
Is so passé
Boring, boring
Boring.

Yellow and black
Is where it's at
Yellow is in
Simple as that
Yellow and black
Is where it's at
Sizzling, sister,
Sizzling!

Seven spots
Is so so-so
So banal
So go-with-the-flow
Seven spots
Is so so-so
Tedious, tedious
Tedious.

Twenty-two spots
Is what I've got
Count them, count them
Hot or what?!
Twenty-two spots
Is what I've got
Dazzling, darling,
Dazzling!

Thea vigintiduopunctata

BUG BOX

COMMON NAME 22-spot Ladybird
SCIENTIFIC NAME *Thea vigintiduopunctata*
FAMILY Coccinellidae
ORDER Coleoptera
CLASS Insecta
PHYLUM Arthropoda
KINGDOM Animalia

ADULTS

SIZE 3–4mm
FAVOURITE FOOD Mildew
LIKE TO BE Grassy places and hedgerows
SEE THEM April to August

FACTABULOUS!

- Most ladybirds eat insects, especially aphids. But the 22-spot Ladybird doesn't.

- The 22-spot Ladybird's favourite food is mildew, which is a kind of fungus.

- The word *vigintiduopunctata* is Latin for '22-spotted'.

2-spot Ladybird

Jo-Jo

Simple

Read my spots:
Less is more
What is all this
Profusion for?

Rein it in
Pare it down
Concentrate
Don't play the clown.

Keep it simple
Keep it true
Back to basics
Back to two.

Two is the essence
Two is chic
Ladybirdness
At its peak.

Adalia bipunctata

BUG BOX

COMMON NAME	2-spot Ladybird
SCIENTIFIC NAME	*Adalia bipunctata*
FAMILY	Coccinellidae
ORDER	Coleoptera
CLASS	Insecta
PHYLUM	Arthropoda
KINGDOM	Animalia

ADULTS

SIZE	3–5mm
FAVOURITE FOOD	Aphids
LIKE TO BE	Almost anywhere
SEE THEM	March to October

FACTABULOUS!

- In winter you might find 2-spot Ladybirds hibernating in your house – especially in the corner of window frames.
- The word *bipunctata* is Latin for '2-spotted'.
- But 2-spot Ladybirds don't always have only two spots ...

2-spot Ladybird

(melanic 6-spot form)

Jimmy

Rebel with six claws
(And six spots)

Turn the world upside down!
Turn the world on its head!
Six is the new two
Black the new red.

Who said rebellion
Was just for teens?
Rebellion is rooted
Deep in my genes.

Adalia bipunctata
(forma sexpustulata)

BUG BOX

COMMON NAME 2-spot Ladybird
(melanic 6-spot form)

SCIENTIFIC NAME *Adalia bipunctata*
(forma sexpustulata)

FAMILY Coccinellidae
ORDER Coleoptera
CLASS Insecta
PHYLUM Arthropoda
KINGDOM Animalia

ADULTS

SIZE 3–5mm
FAVOURITE FOOD Aphids
LIKE TO BE Almost anywhere
SEE THEM March to October

FACTABULOUS!

✤ 2-spot Ladybirds don't always have two spots. Sometimes they have four spots. Sometimes they have six spots. They can even have up to 16 spots!

✤ When 2-spot Ladybirds have four or six spots, the spots aren't black on a red background, but red on a black background.

✤ Ladybirds that have red spots on a black background are called melanic because the substance that makes them black is melanin.

✤ The word *sexpustulata* is Latin for '6-pimpled'.

7-spot Ladybird larva

Luke

Who has a dream

I wish I could fly
I wish I could fly
I wish I could fly away home
I dream at night
Of a world of flight
I wish I could fly away home.

I wish I had wings
I wish I had wings
I wish I had tough, coloured wings
I dream at night
That I'm shiny and bright
I wish I had tough, coloured wings.

But I haven't
I'm squashy and long
With legs either side
I'm all wrong
I'm not polished and twinkly
But drab and all crinkly
The ground must be
Where I belong.

But I wish I could fly
How I wish I could fly
High up into the sky!
I dream all night
That I've mastered flight
Oh, to kiss the earth good-bye ...

Coccinella septempunctata

BUG BOX

COMMON NAME	7-spot Ladybird (larva)
SCIENTIFIC NAME	*Coccinella septempunctata*
FAMILY	Coccinellidae
ORDER	Coleoptera
CLASS	Insecta
PHYLUM	Arthropoda
KINGDOM	Animalia

LARVAE

SIZE	3–8mm
FAVOURITE FOOD	Aphids
LIKE TO BE	Most places where there are aphids
SEE THEM	June and July

FACTABULOUS!

✣ All ladybirds start off as eggs.

✣ The larvae hatch from the eggs, and eat any unhatched eggs around them. Then they start eating lots of aphids.

✣ Over about three weeks, the larvae grow and grow, passing through four stages or 'instars'. At each stage they shed their skin and grow into a bigger one.

✣ After this, the larvae pupate for between five and 14 days, and then emerge as adult ladybirds.

✣ The larvae of the 7-spot Ladybird have eight spots!

✣ Do you know the nursery rhyme 'Ladybird, Ladybird, Fly away home'? I was thinking of that when I wrote this poem.

14-spot Ladybird

Marcus

The golloping gourmet

I'm a very avid aphid eater
Aphids are delish
They're plump and sweet and juicy
Quite the finest dish

I eat aphids for my breakfast
And aphids for my tea
And aphids for my dinner
I'm an aphid devotee

I'm addicted to their texture
Addicted to their taste
Never in my whole life
Have I let one go to waste

My appetite's prodigious
Insatiable, titanic
Here's to scrumptious aphids
Local and organic!

Propylea quatuordecimpunctata

BUG BOX

COMMON NAME	14-spot Ladybird
SCIENTIFIC NAME	*Propylea quatuordecimpunctata*
FAMILY	Coccinellidae
ORDER	Coleoptera
CLASS	Insecta
PHYLUM	Arthropoda
KINGDOM	Animalia

ADULTS

SIZE	3.5–4.5mm
FAVOURITE FOOD	Aphids
LIKE TO BE	Most places
SEE THEM	March to October

FACTABULOUS!

- Gardeners like to have ladybirds in their gardens because they eat lots and lots of aphids, as this ladybird is doing here. Gardeners think aphids are pests.
- Most ladybirds have round spots. But the 14-spot Ladybird often has brick-shaped marks instead of spots, as in this photo.
- The word *quatuordecimpunctata* is Latin for '14-spotted'.

Harlequin Ladybird

Quinn

Unwelcome

Harlequin, Harlequin
Brazen invader in
Danger of slayin'
Your host kith and kin.

Harlequin, Harlequin
You are not welcome in
Blighty, your fightin'
Has us in a spin.

You breed more, you feed more
Indeed your great greed for
Our flesh and our land
Makes us fear we can't win.

Harlequin, Harlequin
Alien harbin-
ger of our demise
Hear this: We'll not give in!

Harmonia axyridis

BUG BOX

COMMON NAME Harlequin Ladybird
SCIENTIFIC NAME *Harmonia axyridis*
FAMILY Coccinellidae
ORDER Coleoptera
CLASS Insecta
PHYLUM Arthropoda
KINGDOM Animalia

ADULTS

SIZE 7–8.5mm

FAVOURITE FOOD Aphids – but also the eggs and larvae of other ladybirds and butterflies, and even adult ladybirds

LIKE TO BE Almost anywhere, especially on trees and low-growing plants like nettles

SEE THEM February to October

FACTABULOUS!

✪ Harlequin Ladybirds have been called 'the most invasive ladybird species on earth'. They come from Asia, and only arrived in Britain in 2004.

✪ Harlequins eat other ladybirds' eggs, larvae and pupae, so they pose a big threat to our native British ladybirds.

✪ One female Harlequin can lay over 1,000 eggs.

✪ Harlequin Ladybirds can be difficult to identify as they come in over 100 different colours and patterns. Look how different the two Harlequins here are, for example.

✪ Over winter, Harlequins sometimes gather in large numbers inside houses and other buildings.

✪ If you see a Harlequin, let the Harlequin Ladybird Survey know. (See 'Over to You' on page 158.)

Eyed Ladybird

Iris

A heavenly sight

Eye, Eye, I've been spotted!
Well you might as well know
I'm the largest ladybird
From tip to toe
In the whole of my family
In the UK
That's the largest
Of 46 species, OK?

Some of my rellies
Have slightly more spots
Some of my rellies
Are wee tiny tots
None can compete
With my statuesque girth
So none can compete
When it comes to brute worth.

But size isn't everything
I'm well aware
Most important of all
Are the halos I bear
Some call them eyes
I think they ain't
I think they're clearly
The marks of a saint.

Anatis ocellata

BUG BOX

COMMON NAME	Eyed Ladybird
SCIENTIFIC NAME	*Anatis ocellata*
FAMILY	Coccinellidae
ORDER	Coleoptera
CLASS	Insecta
PHYLUM	Arthropoda
KINGDOM	Animalia

ADULTS

SIZE	8–10mm
FAVOURITE FOOD	Aphids
LIKE TO BE	In pine trees
SEE THEM	April to August

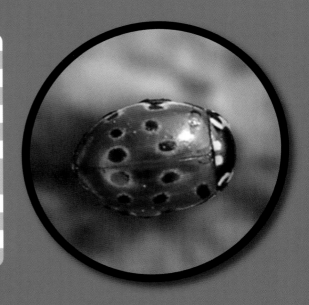

FACTABULOUS!

✣ There are 46 members of the Coccinellidae family in Britain.

✣ Twenty-six of them look like ladybirds – in other words, they are brightly coloured and spotty.

✣ Eyed Ladybirds are the largest ladybirds in Britain.

✣ This is the only Eyed Ladybird I have ever seen. Have you seen one? Or any other species of ladybird? If so, let the UK Ladybird Survey know! (See 'Over to You' on page 158.)

buzz off!

Garden Party

I scuttle
I slither
I skim
I hop

I pitter
I patter
I dangle
and drop.

I flutter
I wriggle
I slink
I slime

I hover
I march
I sucker
and climb.

I shimmy
I creep
I burrow
I dive

I swoop
I crawl
I slow motion
jive.

Arthropods, molluscs
Annelids, all
Ambulant animals
Titchy and small

Out in my garden
Out in yours too
Our very own all-year-round
Miniature zoo.

154

Index

Over to You...

So, now you know what's in and around my garden. But what's in *your* garden? And in your park? And your playing field? The scientists need to know! They can only build up an accurate picture of the wildlife in Britain if we all tell them what animals we see, and where.

How do you tell the scientists what bugs you see? Easy! Go to the BugWatch page of my website, where you'll find links to organisations that record sightings of all sorts of creatures, including butterflies, moths, bees, ladybirds and sawflies.

To find my BugWatch page, go to my website – www.theBigBuzz.biz – and click on the picture of this book.

What happens if you see a creature you don't recognise? No problem! Take a photo of it and upload it to one of the websites listed on my BugWatch page, where experts will identify it for you.

Happy bug watching wherever you are!

www.the**big**buzz.biz

Find Out More...

If you like what you've seen
If you want to know more
My blog and my website
Have plenty in store

There are background stories
And videos
And dates of my upcoming
Live *Buzzing!* shows

There's how I can come
To your school for a day
And how to take pix
In a *Buzzing!* way

Yes, there's photos and info
And feedback and fizz
All at
www.theBigBuzz.biz

Anneliese Emmans Dean

buzz**ing!**

'Anneliese has discovered the poetry in insects. She has the buzz!' Quentin Blake

JUST CLICK ON THE PICTURE OF THIS BOOK!

The End

There's nothing too tiny
Nothing too small
Beetles, butterflies
Bumblebees, all
Are part of the story
With secrets to share
Take the time
To stand and stare ...

Other books in this series:
Feathers and Eggshells – The Bird Journal of a Young London Girl, ISBN 9780954334772
Garden Photo Shoot – A Photographer's Yearbook of Garden Wildlife, ISBN 9780955392832
What's in your Garden? – A Book for Young Explorers, ISBN 9780955392818

www.bramblebybooks.co.uk